Understanding C#12 Coding Standards, Best Practices, and Standards in the Industry

DEVELOPING ROBUST AND MAINTAINABLE CODE IN TODAY'S DEVELOPMENT ENVIRONMENT

Ziggy Rafiq

Website: https://ziggyrafiq.com

LinkedIn: https://www.linkedin.com/in/ziggyrafiq/

GitHub: https://github.com/ziggyrafiq

This publication may not be reproduced, distributed, or transmitted without the prior written permission of the publisher, including photocopying, recording, or other electronic or mechanical methods. Except for brief quotations in critical reviews and certain other non-commercial uses permitted by copyright law, this publication cannot be reproduced, distributed, or transmitted in any form or by any means. While the author/co-author and publisher have made every effort to ensure that this book contains accurate information at press time, they do not assume any liability for any loss, damage, or disruption caused by errors or omissions, regardless of whether such errors or omissions are caused by negligence, accident, or any other reason. The resources in this book are provided for informational purposes only and should not be viewed as a replacement for the specialized training and professional judgment of health care or mental health care professionals. Please always consult a trained professional before making any decisions regarding the treatment of yourself or others. The author/co-author as well as the publisher are not responsible for the use of the information contained in this book.

Copyright © 2024 Ziggy Rafiq

All rights reserved.

ISBN: 9798322695202

Background and Expertise

With over 19 years of experience, Ziggy Rafiq has demonstrated exceptional skills in System Architecture. He has been a full-stack designer and developer for over 19 years. As a Technical Lead Developer in 2004, he demonstrated his leadership and expertise.

It was Ziggy Rafiq's groundbreaking work in 2002 that earned him the Shell Award after he developed an impenetrable login system. At the Microsoft Hero Event in 2008, he was named one of Microsoft's Top 10 Developers in the West Midlands.

Ziggy Rafiq has been recognized as an MVP, VIP, and Member of the Month by C# Corner (March 2024, July 2023), as well as an active speaker and Chapter Lead at the UK Developer Community.

Educational Background

As a student at college, Ziggy Rafiq earned an American Associate Degree in Interactive Multimedia Communication. He obtained a BA Hons in Interactive Multimedia Communication 2:1 from the University of Wolverhampton between 1999 and 2003. Along the way, he acquired a comprehensive understanding of Design, Development, Testing, Deployment, and Project Management, which allowed him to be an effective professional.

Acknowledgement

This book is dedicated to author Ziggy Rafiq's late mother, Mrs. Zubeda Begum, whose unwavering love, support, and encouragement have been a constant source of inspiration for him. Her presence in Ziggy Rafiq's life shaped his journey from January 1st, 1950, to December 1st, 2022, and this book is a tribute to her.

Special Thanks

In creating this book, Ziggy Rafiq would like to extend his sincere gratitude to the following individuals and communities.

Ziggy Rafiq Family and Friends

Throughout the countless hours spent writing this book, I am deeply grateful for my wife and children's support, patience, and understanding.

Ziggy Rafiq Mentors and Advisers

I would like to thank them for their guidance and valuable insights that have enriched the content of this book.

The Web Development Community

As a platform for fostering a vibrant online community of web developers, sharing knowledge, and providing inspiration.

Ziggy Rafiq Late Mother Mrs. Zubeda Begum

A legacy of love and encouragement that continues to inspire Ziggy Rafiq every day.

— Ziggy Rafiq

Table of Content

Chapter 1: Introduction 13
  Importance of Coding Standards 13
  Overview of Best Practices 13
  Evolution of C# Language and Industry Standards 13
  Coding Standards Fundamentals 13
    Understanding the Basics 14
    Consistency and Readability 14
    Scalability and Maintainability 14
  Using Best Practices with C# 14
    Object-Oriented Programming (OOP) Principles 15
    Error Handling and Error Management 15
    Performance Optimization and Memory Management 15
  C# 12 Modern Development Practices 15
    Asynchronous Programming 15
    Functional Programming Features 16
    Test-Driven Development (TDD) and Unit Testing 16
  A Review of Industry Standards and Trends 16
    .NET Ecosystem Integration 16
    Web Development with ASP.NET Core 16
    Xamarin Cross-Platform Development 17
  Examples from Real-World Case Studies 17
    Well-structured and maintainable code examples 17
    Code Refactoring and Performance Optimization Case Studies
    17
    Experts and thought leaders share their insights 17

Key Takeaways 17
   Best Practices and Key Concepts 17
   Coding Standards and Industry Trends Encouraged 17
   Resources for Learning and Staying Current 18
Setting Up Development Environment 19
Chapter 2: Setting Up Development Environment 20
   Choosing the Right IDE 20
      Visual Studio 20
      Visual Studio Code 20
   Configuring Development Tools 21
      Installing .NET SDK 21
      NuGet Package Manager 22
   Version Control Systems 22
      Git 23
      GitHub 23
Coding Standards Fundamentals 24
Chapter 3: Coding Standards Fundamentals 25
   Naming Conventions 25
      Variables and Methods 25
      Classes and Properties 26
   Formatting Guidelines 27
      Indentation and Spacing 27
      Braces Placement 28
   Code Organization 28
      Modularization 29
      Separation of Concerns 30
   Comments and Documentation 32

- XML Documentation Comments 33
  - Inline Comments 35
- Best Practices in C# Programming 36
- Chapter 4: Best Practices in C# Programming 37
  - Object-Oriented Design Principles 37
    - Encapsulation 37
    - Inheritance 38
  - Error Handling and Exception Management 40
    - Try-Catch Blocks 40
    - Custom Exception Classes 41
  - Memory Management and Performance Optimization 43
    - Garbage Collection 44
    - Performance Profiling 45
  - Security Best Practices 46
    - Input Validation 47
    - Authentication and Authorization 48
- Advanced Techniques and Patterns 51
- Chapter 5: Advanced Techniques and Patterns 52
  - Design Patterns in C# 52
    - Singleton Pattern 52
    - Factory Method Pattern 53
  - Asynchronous Programming Patterns 54
    - Async/Await Pattern 55
  - Dependency Injection and Inversion of Control 55
    - Dependency Injection (DI) 56
    - Inversion of Control (IoC) Container 57
  - Unit Testing and Test-Driven Development 58

    Writing Unit Tests 58

    Test-Driven Development (TDD) 60

Integrating with Industry Standards 61

Chapter 6: Integrating with Industry Standards 62

    Compliance with Coding Standards (e.g., Microsoft Guidelines) . 62

    Conforming to Industry Regulations (e.g., GDPR, HIPAA) 63

    Interoperability and Integration Standards 65

    Accessibility Standards and Guidelines 66

Chapter 7: Tooling and Automation 70

    Code Analysis Tools 70

    Continuous Integration/Continuous Deployment (CI/CD) Pipelines 70

    Code Review Practices and Tools 72

    Automated Testing Frameworks 74

Chapter 8: Collaborative Development Practices 78

    Version Control Best Practices 78

    Code Review Processes 78

    Pair Programming and Mob Programming 79

    Agile Development Practices 80

        Scrum 80

        Kanban 81

Collaborative Development Practices 82

Chapter 9: Collaborative Development Practices 83

    Version Control Best Practices 83

        Traceability 83

        Collaboration 83

        Code Quality 83

Commit Regularly	83
Use Descriptive Commit Messages	83
Follow Branching Strategies	84
Meaningful Commit Messages	84
Branching Strategies	84
Frequent Commits	84
Code Review Processes	84
Code Review Processes	84
Quality Assurance	85
Knowledge Sharing	85
Consistency	85
Define Review Criteria	85
Assign Reviewers	85
Use Review Tools	85
Establish Guidelines	86
Provide Constructive Feedback	86
Utilize Code Review Tools	86
Provide Constructive Feedback	86
Pair Programming and Mob Programming	86
Knowledge Sharing	86
Enhanced Code Quality	87
Improved Collaboration	87
Rotate Roles	87
Establish Clear Goals	87
Encourage Communication	87
Use Collaboration Tools	87
Pair Programming	88

- Mob Programming 88
- Agile Development Practices 88
  - Flexibility 88
  - Transparency 88
  - Iterative Delivery 89
  - Define Clear Objectives 89
  - Embrace Empirical Process Control 89
  - Foster Cross-Functional Teams 89
  - Iterate and Improve 89
  - Embrace Agile Principles 89
  - Scrum Framework 90
  - Kanban Method 90
- Chapter 10: Case Studies and Examples 92
  - Real-world Examples of Good and Bad Practices 92
    - Why Use Real-world Examples 92
    - How to Use the Real-world Examples 92
    - Good Practice 93
    - Bad Practices 93
  - Refactoring Exercises 94
    - Why Use Refactoring Exercises 94
    - How to Use Refactoring Exercises 94
    - Identify Code Smells 95
    - Refactoring Techniques 95
    - Before-and-After Examples 95
  - Performance Optimization Case Studies 96
    - Why Use Performance Optimization Case Studies 96
    - How to Use Performance Optimization Case Studies 97

Chapter 11: Future Trends and Evolving Standard 101
Emerging Technologies in C# Ecosystem 101
NET 6 and Beyond 101
Blazor and WebAssembly 101
Cloud-Native Development 101
Potential Changes in Coding Standards and Practices 101
Shift towards Functional Programming 102
Emphasis on Clean Code Principles 102
Adoption of AI and Machine Learning 102
Adapting to Future Industry Trends 102
Continuous Learning and Upskilling 102
Agile and DevOps Practices 103
Ethical and Responsible AI 103
Chapter 12: Wrapping Up 105
Recap of Key Takeaways 105
Coding Standards and Best Practices 105
Collaborative Development 105
Adaptation to Future Trends 105
Final Thoughts on Achieving Code Quality 105
Resources for Further Learning 106

1
Introduction

Overview

In C# software development, it is important to adhere to coding standards and best practices. If teams ensure code quality, readability, and maintainability, they can collaborate effectively, streamline code reviews, and minimize errors. Object-oriented programming principles, error handling, performance optimization, and modern development practices such as asynchronous programming and test-driven development are among the concepts covered in depth. The importance of staying current with industry standards and trends is underscored by real-world case studies and insights from industry experts. For developers to produce high-quality C# code and advance in their careers, they need to follow coding standards, adopt best practices, and engage in continuous learning.

You can access or download the code from my GitHub Repository
https://github.com/ziggyrafiq/CSharp12-Coding-Standards-Best-Practices-Industry

Chapter 1: Introduction
Importance of Coding Standards
Adhering to coding standards is essential in modern software development to ensure code quality, readability, and maintainability. Teams can collaborate more effectively, code reviews are streamlined, and bugs and errors are less likely to be introduced when coding standards are consistent. Code that is written according to established coding conventions is easier to understand, debug, and extend, resulting in more efficient development cycles and higher-quality software.

Overview of Best Practices
C# programming best practices include a broad range of principles and techniques that ensure high-quality, efficient, and maintainable code. In addition to following object-oriented design principles, such as encapsulation, inheritance, and polymorphism, modern development practices include asynchronous programming, functional programming, and test-driven development (TDD). These best practices can help developers produce code that is more robust, scalable, and adaptable to changing needs.

Evolution of C# Language and Industry Standards
With each new version of the C# programming language, new features, enhancements, and improvements are introduced that aim to make development more efficient and productive. The evolution of C# has coincided with the evolution of industry standards and best practices, influenced by technological advancements, development methodologies, and industry trends. Staying current with best practices and utilizing the full capabilities of C# in today's development landscape requires understanding C#'s evolution and industry standards.

Coding Standards Fundamentals
As a software developer, it is imperative to learn about C# Coding Standards Fundamentals to ensure consistency, readability, and maintainability. Among these standards are naming conventions, code formatting guidelines, and documentation practices. For example, C# uses camelCase for variables and methods, and PascalCase for classes. Code clarity and comprehension are further enhanced by consistent indentation, spacing, and comments. These fundamentals can help developers create

more efficient development cycles and higher-quality software products by making codebases easier to understand, debug, and modify.

Understanding the Basics

Among the established coding standards that developers should follow are naming conventions, code formatting guidelines, and documentation practices for maintaining consistency and readability in codebases. C#, for instance, uses camelCase naming conventions for variables and methods, while PascalCase is used for classes. Consistent indentation, spacing, and comments also improve readability and comprehension of code.

Consistency and Readability

To enhance the readability and maintainability of code, coding styles must be consistent across teams and projects. By adopting a unified coding style and using meaningful names for variables, methods, and classes, developers reduce cognitive overhead and improve code clarity. Indenting, formatting, and commenting improve readability and comprehension, making code easier to understand and modify for developers.

Scalability and Maintainability

A well-maintained codebase follows principles such as separation of concerns, encapsulation, and abstractions, and is modular, encapsulated, and organized. By breaking down complex systems into manageable components, modularization improves scalability and maintainability. Code maintenance and dependency reduction are improved by encapsulating implementation details and showing only relevant interfaces. Additionally, writing self-documenting code reduces the need for extensive comments and improves the readability and maintainability of the code.

Using Best Practices with C#

C# Best Practices are essential to producing high-quality, efficient, and maintainable code. A variety of principles and techniques are included in these practices, including asynchronous programming, functional programming, and test-driven development. By following these best practices, developers can write code that is robust, scalable, and adaptable to changing requirements. Best practices ensure that C# applications are well-designed, performant, and easy to maintain over time, resulting in improved development outcomes.

Object-Oriented Programming (OOP) Principles

Object-oriented programming (OOP) principles help developers design and implement software systems based on objects, classes, and inheritance. OOP is based on the concepts of encapsulation, inheritance, and polymorphism. Inheritance allows classes to inherit the properties and behaviours of parent classes by bundling data and methods in a class, ensuring data integrity and hiding implementation details. Encapsulation ensures data integrity and hides implementation details. It enhances the flexibility and extensibility of code by allowing objects to take on multiple forms.

Error Handling and Error Management

Robust and reliable software needs to be able to handle exceptions gracefully. C# offers robust exception-handling mechanisms through try-catch blocks. Developers can prevent application crashes and provide meaningful error messages to users by handling exceptions effectively. Additionally, custom exception classes and logging frameworks can improve error management and debugging.

Performance Optimization and Memory Management

High-performance applications require efficient memory management and performance optimization. C# features automatic memory management through garbage collection, which deals with unused memory and prevents memory leaks. By minimizing memory allocations, reducing unnecessary object creation, and using asynchronous programming for I/O-bound operations, developers can optimize performance. An application's performance can be improved by using profiling tools to identify performance bottlenecks and optimize critical sections

C# 12 Modern Development Practices

Asynchronous Programming

In asynchronous programming, developers can write non-blocking, responsive applications that handle concurrent operations efficiently and non-blocking. The Task Parallel Library (TPL) and async/await keywords in C# 12 simplify asynchronous code development and improve scalability and responsiveness while simplifying asynchronous programming.

Functional Programming Features
Using C#, developers can write concise and expressive code using functional programming features. Developers can write functional-style code using lambda expressions and LINQ (Language-Integrated Query), emphasizing immutability and declarative programming. Code clarity, maintainability, and testability are enhanced by immutable data structures and functional composition.

Test-Driven Development (TDD) and Unit Testing
A test-driven development (TDD) methodology emphasizes the importance of writing automated tests before writing actual code. By writing tests first, developers clarify requirements, design modular, testable code, and ensure code correctness. The correctness, reliability, and maintainability of C# code can be ensured by writing unit tests using testing frameworks like NUnit or MSTest.

A Review of Industry Standards and Trends
.NET Ecosystem Integration
C# integrates seamlessly with the broader .NET ecosystem, including libraries, frameworks, and tools. For cross-platform development, developers can use .NET Standard and .NET Core, ensuring interoperability and compatibility across different environments. Developers can leverage existing codebases and libraries by leveraging interoperability with other .NET languages like VB.NET and F#.

Web Development with ASP.NET Core
Modern web applications and APIs can be built using C# using ASP.NET Core, a powerful framework. A web application can be scalable and maintainable using ASP.NET Core MVC, which offers robust support for front-end development using Razor Pages and Blazor. Further scalability, reliability, and performance can be enhanced by integrating Azure with other cloud platforms.

Xamarin Cross-Platform Development
With Xamarin, developers can write code once and deploy it across multiple platforms, including iOS and Android. Using Xamarin, developers can build cross-platform mobile applications using C#. By sharing code between desktop and mobile platforms, development time and effort are reduced, allowing for faster time-to-market and better code reuse.

Examples from Real-World Case Studies
Well-structured and maintainable code examples
The results of adhering to coding standards and best practices are well-structured, maintainable codebases, as demonstrated by case studies. Using coding standards and best practices, developers solve complex problems, enhance code quality, and increase development efficiency in real-world examples.

Code Refactoring and Performance Optimization Case Studies
The benefits of code refactoring and performance optimization for maintainability, readability, and performance are illustrated in case studies. As a result of refactoring and optimization techniques, software quality and performance are improved, as real-world examples highlight common code smells and performance bottlenecks.

Experts and thought leaders share their insights
It is possible to gain valuable insights into emerging trends, best practices, and challenges in C# development through interviews with industry experts and thought leaders. Keeping up with today's development landscape requires mastering C# coding standards, best practices, and industry standards, as experts share their experiences, tips, and recommendations.

Key Takeaways
Best Practices and Key Concepts
Emphasize the need for robust and maintainable C# code by summarizing key concepts, coding standards, and best practices covered in the chapter.

Coding Standards and Industry Trends Encouraged
Improve code quality, readability, and maintainability by encouraging developers to adhere to coding standards, best practices, and industry trends.

Resources for Learning and Staying Current

Maintain developers' knowledge of C# development trends, best practices, and industry standards by providing resources for further learning, such as books, online courses, and community forums. To master C# programming and excel in their careers, encourage continuous learning and professional development.

2
Setting Up Development Environment

Overview

The chapter delves into the critical process of Choosing the Right IDE for C# development, emphasizing its pivotal role in enhancing productivity and efficiency. Visual Studio and Visual Studio Code are considered comprehensive options with extensive support and versatile features when it comes to code completion, debugging tools, and integration with version control systems. It also emphasizes the importance of Configuring Development Tools to streamline the development process and optimize workflow, covering components such as compilers, build systems, and package managers. It also discussed how Version Control Systems (VCS) can be integrated into development workflows, emphasizing Git's importance in managing code changes and facilitating collaboration. To ensure seamless coding and collaboration in C# development projects, developers can follow these insights and recommendations to set up their development environment efficiently, choose the right tools, and configure essential components.

Chapter 2: Setting Up Development Environment

Choosing the Right IDE
Choosing the Right IDE for C# development is crucial for maximizing productivity and efficiency. Considerations include code completion, debugging tools, and integration with version control systems. Visual Studio and Visual Studio Code provide comprehensive support for C# development, along with a rich ecosystem of extensions and plugins. In order to facilitate smoother development workflows and better outcomes, developers should evaluate IDEs according to compatibility with project requirements, ease of use, and community support.

Visual Studio
C# programming can be done using Visual Studio IDE, a comprehensive development environment.

We can utilize IntelliSense for code completion, debugging tools, and project templates for a wide range of applications.

```
Console.WriteLine("Hello, from Ziggy Rafiq!");
```

Visual Studio Code
The Visual Studio Code IDE comes with extensive support for C# and is lightweight and versatile.

Add IntelliSense, debugging, and an integrated terminal to VS Code by installing the C# extension.

```
Console.WriteLine("Hello, from Ziggy Rafiq!");
```

Configuring Development Tools

Optimizing workflow and streamlining the development process requires the configuration of Development Tools for C#. To ensure smooth code compilation, testing, and deployment, it is important to set up tools such as compilers, build systems, and package managers. Developers should customize settings and extensions to meet project requirements and personal preferences, whether they are using integrated development environments (IDEs) like Visual Studio or lightweight editors like Visual Studio Code. Moreover, integrating tools with continuous integration pipelines and version control systems improves collaboration and automation. By effectively configuring development tools, developers can increase productivity, improve code quality, and deliver high-quality C# applications efficiently.

Installing .NET SDK

We can use the .NET SDK to build, run, and deploy C# applications on a variety of platforms by downloading and installing it.

The following commands can be used to verify installation:

```
dotnet --version
```

The image below will show us the Windows command console whereby we have typed the dontnet --version to verify the .NET SDK installation.

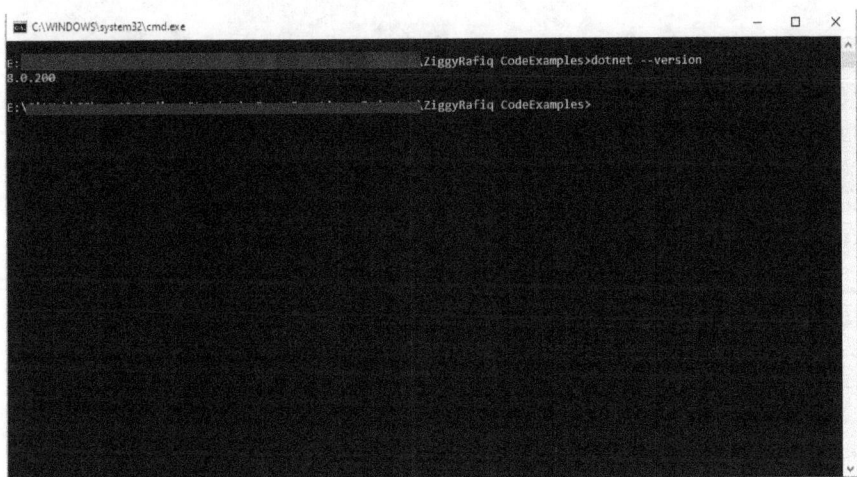

NuGet Package Manager

In C# projects, configure NuGet package manager to manage dependencies.

The Package Manager UI or the NuGet Package Manager Console can be used to install packages.

```
dotnet add package Newtonsoft.Json
```

The image below demonstrates how to install the package via the Windows Command line by navigating to the project folder and then typing dotnet add package Newtonsoft.Json.

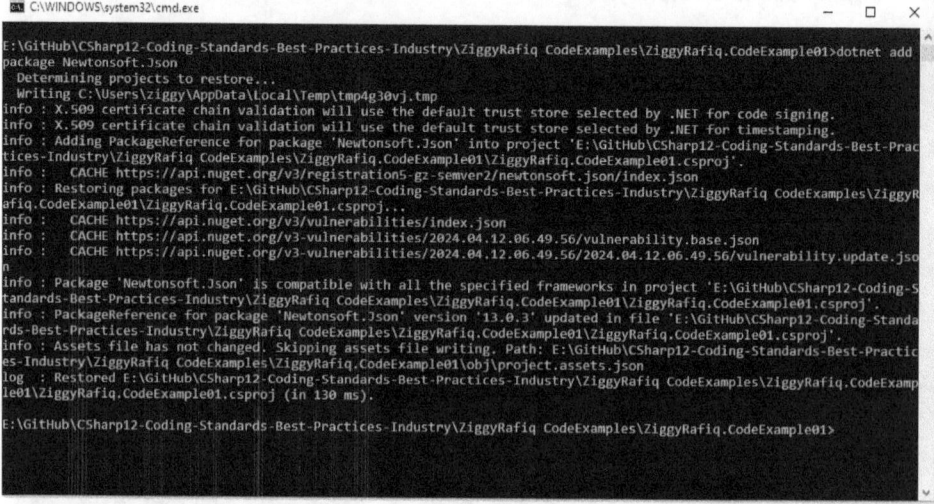

Version Control Systems

C# development projects require Version Control Systems (VCS) for managing code changes and facilitating collaboration. By using a VCS like Git, developers can manage project versions efficiently, track changes, collaborate effectively, and track changes. Parallel development and team collaboration are possible while maintaining code integrity with features like branching, merging, and conflict resolution. By integrating a version control system into development workflows, code reviews are streamlined, deployment processes are streamlined, and a history of changes is provided. In addition to enhancing productivity, version control systems enable C# developers to ensure code quality and manage software projects effectively.

Git
Using Git for version control and collaboration on C# projects is recommended.

For tracking changes and managing project history, set up a Git repository.

```
git init

git add .

git commit -m "My Initial commit"
```

GitHub
For hosting C# projects, create a GitHub account and set up remote repositories.

The features of GitHub enable we to collaborate with team members, manage branches, and track issues.

```
git remote add origin <repository_url>

git push -u origin master
```

Developers can set up their development environment efficiently, choose the right tools for C# development, and configure essential components to ensure seamless coding and collaboration by following these steps.

3

Coding Standards Fundamentals

Overview

To ensure consistency, clarity, and maintainability in C# development projects, Chapter 3: Coding Standards Fundamentals provides a solid foundation. Starting with Naming Conventions, developers adhere to guidelines, promoting a cohesive, comprehensible codebase necessary for efficient collaboration and scalability. In addition to enhancing code readability and reducing cognitive load, Formatting Guidelines provide structure. The organization emphasizes logical structuring to facilitate future modifications and scalability. Comments and Documentation emphasize the importance of clear code documentation, which makes it easier to understand and collaborate as well as ensuring project viability. In C#, these fundamentals help developers make codebases easier to understand, collaborate on, and maintain, resulting in higher-quality software products.

Chapter 3: Coding Standards Fundamentals

Naming Conventions

To ensure consistency and clarity in variable, method, and class names, developers adhere to established guidelines in Coding Standards Fundamentals for C#'s Naming Conventions section. Code can be read and maintained more easily by following conventions such as camelCase for variables and methods and PascalCase for classes. Developers need to maintain consistency in their naming practices to promote a cohesive and comprehensible codebase that promotes efficient collaboration and facilitates future maintenance and scalability.

Variables and Methods

To name variables and methods in C#, follow the camelCase convention.

```csharp
int personAge = 28;


void displayPersonAge()
{
    // Method implementation

    Console.WriteLine($"Person age is {personAge}");

}
```

Classes and Properties
For classes and properties, use PascalCase naming convention.

```csharp
namespace ZiggyRafiq.CodeExample02;
public class PersonDetials
{
    public Guid Id { get; set; }
    public string FirstName { get; set; } = string.Empty;
    public string LastName { get; set; } = string.Empty;
    public int Age { get; set; }

    public string FullName
    {
        get
        {
            return $"{FirstName} {LastName}";
        }
    }
}
```

Formatting Guidelines
Providing guidelines on how to structure code for readability and maintainability is part of the Coding Standards Fundamentals for C#. When code elements are consistently indented, spaced, and aligned, developers are able to understand and modify it more efficiently. By adhering to formatting guidelines, codebases are uniform, facilitating collaboration and reducing cognitive load. Following these guidelines results in easier-to-understand, easier-to-debug, and easier-to-maintain code, leading to more efficient development cycles and higher-quality software.

Indentation and Spacing
Improve the readability of our code by using consistent indentation (usually four spaces) and spacing.

```csharp
namespace ZiggyRafiq.CodeExample02;

public class Extensions
{
    public void ExmpleOneMethod()
    {
        bool condition = true; // Placeholder condition, replace with your actual condition

        if (condition)
        {
            Console.WriteLine("Indented code block");
        }
        else
        {
            Console.WriteLine("Condition is false");
        }
    }
}
```

Braces Placement

The opening braces should be placed on the same line as the statement, and the closing braces should be placed on a separate line.

```
if (condition)

{

   // Code block

   Console.WriteLine("Condition is true");

}
else

{

   // Code block if condition is false

   Console.WriteLine("Condition is false");

}
```

Code Organization

As part of Coding Standards Fundamentals for C#, developers establish practices for structuring code that enhances clarity and maintainability. Developers improve readability and facilitate future modifications by logically organizing code into modules, namespaces, classes, and methods. By keeping codebases consistent, collaboration becomes simpler and errors are less common. A systematic approach to development is promoted by adhering to code organization standards, which promotes efficient code maintenance and scalability.

Modularization
Maintainability and scalability will be improved by organizing code into logical modules and classes.

```csharp
// Example of modularization
namespace ZiggyRafiq.CodeExample02;
// Define a class to encapsulate related functionality
public class ExampleClass
{
    // Class implementation

    // Example method within the class
    public void EampleMethod()
    {
        // Method implementation
        Console.WriteLine("EampleMethod() is executed.");
    }
}
// We can define more classes or modules within the same namespace
public class AnotherExampleClass
{
    // Class implementation

    // Example method within the class
    public void AnotherExampleMethod()
    {
        // Method implementation
```

```
        Console.WriteLine("AnotherExampleMethod() is executed.");
    }
}
```

Separation of Concerns

Make sure that different concerns (such as presentation, business logic, data access) are separated into distinct modules.

```
// Example of modularization
// Define the presentation layer
namespace ZiggyRafiq.CodeExample02;
// Define a class responsible for presenting data or interacting with the user interface
    public class PresentationClass
    {
        // Presentation logic implementation
        // Example method within the class
        public void DisplayMessage(string message)
        {
            // Method implementation to display a message to the user
            Console.WriteLine(message);
        }
    }


// Define the business logic layer
namespace ZiggyRafiq.CodeExample02;
// Define a class responsible for handling business logic
```

```csharp
public class BusinessLogicClass
{
    // Business logic implementation
    // Example method within the class
    public void ProcessData(int data)
    {
        // Method implementation to process data according to business rules
        Console.WriteLine($"Processing data: {data}");
    }
}


// Define the data access layer
namespace ZiggyRafiq.CodeExample02;
// Define a class responsible for data access operations
public class DataAccessClass
{
    // Data access logic implementation

    // Example method within the class
    public void GetData()
    {
        // Method implementation to retrieve data from a data source
        Console.WriteLine("Getting data from the database.");
    }
}
```

This completion separates the concerns into distinct modules by creating three namespaces: PresentationLayer, BusinessLogicLayer, and DataAccessLayer. Since each namespace contains classes for addressing specific concerns: presentation, business logic, and data access, it allows for better organization and maintainability of the codebase.

Comments and Documentation

In the Coding Standards Fundamentals for C#, the importance of clear and informative code documentation is emphasized under Comments and Documentation. The development process enhances the readability and maintainability of code by incorporating comments strategically throughout the codebase and providing comprehensive documentation for methods, classes, and modules. Code segments are clarified with comments, making them easier to understand and facilitate future modifications. Insights into the architecture and functionality of the codebase can be gained from comprehensive documentation, resulting in smoother collaboration and shortened onboarding times for new team members. The longevity and sustainability of C# projects are ensured by prioritizing comments and documentation.

XML Documentation Comments

Classes, methods, and properties can be documented using XML documentation comments.

```csharp
namespace ZiggyRafiq.CodeExample02;

/// <summary>
/// Represents a person.
/// </summary>
public class Person
{
    /// <summary>
    /// Gets or sets the person's name.
    /// </summary>
    public string Name { get; set; }


    /// <summary>
    /// Initializes a new instance of the <see cref="Person"/> class.
    /// </summary>
    public Person()
    {
        // Default constructor
    }


    /// <summary>
    /// Initializes a new instance of the <see cref="Person"/> class with the specified name.
    /// </summary>
    /// <param name="name">The name of the person.</param>
```

```csharp
    public Person(string name)
    {
        Name = name;
    }

    /// <summary>
    /// Gets the person's name.
    /// </summary>
    /// <returns>The name of the person.</returns>
    public string GetName()
    {
        return Name;
    }

    /// <summary>
    /// Sets the person's name.
    /// </summary>
    /// <param name="name">The name of the person.</param>
    public void SetName(string name)
    {
        Name = name;
    }
}
```

In this completion, each class, method, and property is meticulously documented using XML documentation comments. These comments serve to elucidate the purpose and usage of the corresponding code elements. Utilizing tags such as <summary> for brief descriptions, <param> for method and constructor parameters, <returns> for method return values, and <see cref=""/> for referencing other code elements, the documentation systematically conveys essential information. Such comprehensive XML documentation comments not only facilitate better understanding of the codebase but also enable documentation generators and integrated development environments (IDEs) to automatically generate comprehensive documentation for the code.

Inline Comments

Code sections with complex or non-obvious complexity should be clarified with inline comments.

```csharp
// Calculate the total price
decimal quantity = 12; // Example quantity
decimal price = 8.99m; // Example price
decimal totalPrice = quantity * price; // Calculate the total price
Console.WriteLine($"Total Price: {totalPrice:C2}");
```

In this code example above, we have three variables: quantity, which represents the quantity of items being purchased; price, which represents the cost per item; and totalPrice, which calculates the total cost by multiplying the quantity by the price. The total cost for the items being purchased can be calculated by making adjustments to quantity and price. This allows for a flexible calculation of the total cost based on different quantities and prices per item.

It is important to follow these coding standards fundamentals to ensure consistency, readability, and maintainability of C# codebases so that developers can collaborate and understand them more easily.

4

Best Practices in C# Programming

Overview

The chapter on Object-Oriented Design Principles provides a foundational understanding of key principles for mastering best practices in C# programming. As well as providing data integrity and modularity, encapsulation promotes code reuse and extensibility through inheritance. By enabling dynamic behaviour and flexibility, polymorphism makes software systems modular, maintainable, and scalable. The sections on Error Handling and Exception Management emphasize the importance of anticipating and gracefully handling unexpected situations during program execution, which are critical aspects of robust C# programming. We explore Memory Management and Performance Optimization as vital components of efficient C# programming, with a focus on optimizing memory usage and maximizing application performance and efficiency. Lastly, Security Best Practices are highlighted to protect applications from vulnerabilities and unauthorized access, emphasizing input validation, authentication, authorization, and regular updates to address known security vulnerabilities. A C# application that meets the needs of modern software development can be resilient, secure, and high-performance by incorporating these principles and practices.

Chapter 4: Best Practices in C# Programming

Object-Oriented Design Principles

Encapsulating data and behaviour within classes, inheritance for code reuse, and polymorphism for flexibility are key principles to mastering best practices in C# programming. By encapsulating data and enforcing modularity, inheritance facilitates code reuse and hierarchical relationships, while polymorphism enables objects to take on multiple forms, enabling dynamic behaviour and extensibility. Object-oriented programming in C# can be embodied by applying these principles effectively, resulting in modular, maintainable, and scalable software systems.

Encapsulation

The implementation details of classes should be hidden from external code, so data and behaviour can be encapsulated within them.

```csharp
namespace ZiggyRafiq.CodeExample03.Encapsulation;

public class Car
{
    private string _model;

    public string Model
    {
        get { return _model; }
        private set
        {
            // Add validation if necessary
            _model = value;
        }
    }
}
```

```
public Car(string model)
{
    Model = model; // Using the property setter for encapsulation
}
}
```

In this code example above, the Model property has a private setter, ensuring that it can only be set within the Car class itself. This helps to encapsulate the data within the class, so that external code cannot modify it directly. A constructor is also added to initialize the Model property upon object creation, still using the property setter for encapsulation. The class can be extended to encapsulate more data and behavior by adding more methods.

Inheritance
Inheritance promotes code reuse and extensibility by creating hierarchies of related classes.

```csharp
namespace ZiggyRafiq.CodeExample03.Inheritance;
public class Animal
{
    public void Eat()
    {
        Console.WriteLine("Animal is eating.");
    }
}

namespace ZiggyRafiq.CodeExample03.Inheritance;
public class Dog : Animal
{
    public void Bark()
    {
        Console.WriteLine("Dog is barking.");
    }
}


using ZiggyRafiq.CodeExample03.Inheritance;


Console.WriteLine("Hello, from Ziggy Rafiq!");

//Inheritance Code Example
Dog dog = new Dog();
dog.Eat();  // Inherited method from Animal class
dog.Bark(); // Method specific to Dog class
```

A common behavior among animals is represented by the method Eat() in this code example. Dog inherits from Animal and has access to the Eat() method. Additionally, Dog introduces a method called Bark() that is specific to dogs. A Dog instance is instantiated in the Main method, which allows it to invoke both inherited (Eat()) and specific (Bark()) methods, demonstrating the principles of inheritance.

Error Handling and Exception Management

Exception Management and Error Handling are critical aspects of robust C# programming practices. Error handling involves anticipating and gracefully handling unexpected situations during program execution. It is possible to prevent crashes and provide meaningful feedback to users by employing error-handling techniques.

Exception management lets developers identify, capture, and handle exceptions systematically. An exception is thrown when an exceptional condition occurs, such as division by zero or the absence of a file. The code within the try block is monitored for exceptions, and control is transferred to the catch block for handling if any occur. Developers use try-catch blocks to handle exceptions.

By gracefully handling errors, preventing application crashes, and providing informative error messages to users, exception management improves the reliability and robustness of C# applications. It is possible to build more resilient and user-friendly software by anticipating potential failure points and implementing appropriate exception-handling strategies.

Try-Catch Blocks

Try-catch blocks can be used to handle exceptions gracefully and prevent application crashes.

```
//Try-Catch Blocks Code Example One

try

{

    // Code that may throw an exception

    int x = 10;

    int y = 0;
```

```csharp
    int result = x / y; // Division by zero will throw an exception
    Console.WriteLine($"Result: {result}");
}
catch (Exception ex)
{
    // Handle exception
    Console.WriteLine($"An error occurred: {ex.Message}");
}
```

As shown in the code example above, we try to execute code that may throw an exception within the try block. A DivideByZeroException occurs when we divide an integer by zero. The control is immediately transferred to the catch block if an exception occurs. During the catch block, we print out the error message associated with the exception. While in this case, we simply printed the message, you can implement more sophisticated error handling logic if necessary. If the code encounters the division by zero exception, it gracefully transitions to the catch block, which then displays an error message detailing the reason for the exception.

Custom Exception Classes

To represent specific error conditions in your application, you can define custom exception classes.

```csharp
namespace ZiggyRafiq.CodeExample03;

// Custom exception class representing a specific error condition
public class CustomException : Exception
{
    public CustomException(string message) : base(message)
    {
```

```csharp
    }
}

//Try-Catch Blocks Code Example Two
try
{
    // Code that may throw an exception
    int age = -5;
    if (age < 0)
    {
        throw new CustomException("Age cannot be negative.");
    }
    Console.WriteLine($"Age: {age}");
}
catch (CustomException ex)
{
    // Handle custom exception
    Console.WriteLine($"Custom Exception: {ex.Message}");
}
catch (Exception ex)
{
    // Handle other exceptions
    Console.WriteLine($"An error occurred: {ex.Message}");
}
```

This code example above we shows how we define a custom exception class called CustomException, which inherits from the base Exception class, allowing us to represent specific error conditions within our application. The Main method's try block validates the age, throwing a CustomException with the appropriate error message if it is negative. In the event that a CustomException is thrown, it is caught by the catch block, where its message is displayed. Furthermore, a generic catch block handles other exceptions not explicitly caught. Upon encountering a negative age during runtime, the code throws a CustomException, triggering the appropriate catch block to display the appropriate error message.

Memory Management and Performance Optimization

Memory Management and Performance Optimization are vital components of efficient C# programming. Memory management involves allocating and dealing with memory resources to prevent memory leaks and ensure optimal usage. Memory is automatically managed by garbage collection in C#, which identifies and releases unused memory periodically. Optimizing memory usage and preventing performance bottlenecks can be accomplished by minimizing memory allocations, reducing unnecessary object creation, and managing object lifetimes effectively.

As part of performance optimization, C# applications are optimized for speed and efficiency. I/O-bound operations can be enhanced by optimizing algorithm efficiency, reducing unnecessary computations, and using asynchronous programming. Developers can also use profiling tools to identify performance bottlenecks, which allows them to optimize critical code sections.

If memory management and performance optimization are prioritized, developers can create C# applications that are not only fast and efficient but also scalable and reliable, meeting user expectations and ensuring positive user experiences.

Garbage Collection

To prevent memory leaks and improve application stability, let the .NET garbage collector manage memory automatically.

```csharp
//Garbage Collection Code Example

// Allocate memory for a large object
byte[] largeObject = new byte[1000000];

// Indicate to the garbage collector that now would be a good time to collect garbage.
GC.Collect();

// Display total memory allocated for the program
long memoryAllocated = GC.GetTotalMemory(true);
Console.WriteLine($"Total memory allocated: {memoryAllocated} bytes");
```

With GC.Collect(), the garbage collector is prompted to collect garbage for a large object. It retrieves the total allocated memory by using GC.GetTotalMemory(true) and prints it out. The GC.Collect() function is not often necessary, but it serves as an example here. This illustrates the importance of garbage collection for memory management, improving application stability and reducing memory leaks.

The garbage collector will run automatically when needed in most cases, so you shouldn't have to manually call GC.Collect(); in most cases. In some situations, however, it might be necessary to explicitly call it, such as when dealing with large amounts of memory or long-running processes.

Performance Profiling
Make use of performance profiling tools to identify bottlenecks and optimize critical code sections.

```csharp
//Performance Profiling Code Example

// Create a Stopwatch instance
Stopwatch stopwatch = new Stopwatch();

// Start the stopwatch
stopwatch.Start();

// Code section to be profiled
for (int i = 0; i < 1000000; i++)
{
    // Simulate some operation
    double result = Math.Sqrt(i);
}

// Stop the stopwatch
stopwatch.Stop();

// Display elapsed time
Console.WriteLine($"Elapsed time: {stopwatch.ElapsedMilliseconds} milliseconds");
```

With the line Stopwatch stopwatch = new Stopwatch();, we first create a Stopwatch object. When the stopwatch is started, we call stopwatch.Start(); to signal its start. Following this, we execute the code section we wish to profile, which may involve performing mathematical operations through a loop. Once the intended code segment concludes, we halt the stopwatch via stopwatch.Stop();, marking the end of the time measurement. Finally, to view the elapsed time, we access the ElapsedMilliseconds property of the Stopwatch instance, which provides the duration in milliseconds. This series of steps enables efficient profiling of code execution time, aiding in performance analysis and optimization efforts.

Using dedicated profiling tools like JetBrains dotTrace, Visual Studio Profiler, or PerfView, you can measure the execution time of a specific code section in this example. For more comprehensive performance profiling, consider JetBrains dotTrace. For analyzing performance bottlenecks and optimizing critical code sections, these tools offer more advanced features.

Security Best Practices

C# programming relies heavily on security best practices to protect applications from vulnerabilities and unauthorized access. Security measures help safeguard sensitive data, prevent unauthorized modifications, and mitigate security threats. Input validation, parameterized queries, and encryption all protect data in transit and at rest from injection attacks.

Not only this implementing authentication and authorization mechanisms ensures that only authorized users can access certain functionalities or data within the application. In addition to avoiding hardcoded credentials, secure password hashing algorithms enhance overall application security.

It is also important to update dependencies, libraries, and frameworks regularly to address known security vulnerabilities. C# developers can protect users' data and privacy by integrating security into the development lifecycle and staying abreast of emerging threats and security best practices.

Input Validation
Ensure input data is validated to prevent security vulnerabilities such as SQL injection and cross-site scripting (XSS).

```csharp
using Microsoft.Data.SqlClient;

/Input Validation Code Example

// Simulated user input
string userInput = "<script>alert('XSS attack');</script>";

// Validate input to prevent XSS
string sanitizedInput = HttpUtility.HtmlEncode(userInput);

// Simulated SQL query
string sqlQuery = "SELECT * FROM Users WHERE Username = @Username";

// Create SQL connection and command
using (SqlConnection connection = new SqlConnection("connectionString"))
{
    using (SqlCommand command = new SqlCommand(sqlQuery, connection))
    {
        // Validate input to prevent SQL injection
        command.Parameters.AddWithValue("@Username", sanitizedInput);

        // Execute SQL command
        connection.Open();
        SqlDataReader reader = command.ExecuteReader();
        while (reader.Read())
        {
            // Process data
        }
```

```
        }
    }
```

In the code example above, we first simulate user input (userInput) potentially containing XSS attack code. Using HttpUtility.HtmlEncode(), we encode HTML special characters in order to prevent XSS attacks. Afterward, we simulate a SQL query (sqlQuery) using the user input as a parameter. In order to prevent SQL injection attacks, we use parameterized queries (command.Parameters.AddWithValue()), which treat user input as data rather than executable code, thereby enhancing security.

Authentication and Authorization

Access to sensitive resources should be controlled through authentication and authorization mechanisms.

```csharp
//Authentication and Authorization Code Example
// Simulated user credentials
string username = "user123";
string password = "password123";
// Simulated user input
string userInputUsername = Console.ReadLine();
string userInputPassword = Console.ReadLine();
// Simulated user roles
string[] userRoles = { "Admin", "User" };
// Perform authentication
bool isAuthenticated = AuthenticateUser(username, password, userInputUsername, userInputPassword);

if (isAuthenticated)
```

```csharp
{
    // Perform authorization
    bool isAuthorized = AuthorizeUser(userRoles, "Admin");

    if (isAuthorized)
    {
        // Access granted to sensitive resource
        Console.WriteLine("Access granted to sensitive resource.");
    }
    else
    {
        // User is not authorized
        Console.WriteLine("Access denied: User is not authorized to access this resource.");
    }
}
else
{
    // Authentication failed
    Console.WriteLine("Authentication failed: Invalid username or password.");
}

static bool AuthenticateUser(string expectedUsername, string expectedPassword, string userInputUsername, string userInputPassword)
{
    return expectedUsername == userInputUsername && expectedPassword ==
```

```
userInputPassword;
}


static bool AuthorizeUser(string[] userRoles, string requiredRole)
{
    return Array.Exists(userRoles, role => role == requiredRole);
}
```

To authenticate, we simulate user credentials (username and password) and prompt the user for input (userInputUsername and userInputPassword). Additionally, we simulate user roles (userRoles) and perform authentication by comparing provided credentials with expected ones using the AuthenticateUser method. Using the AuthorizeUser method, we verify if the user has the required role to access a sensitive resource. Access to the sensitive resource is granted or denied based on the authentication and authorization outcomes.

Modern software development demands robust, secure, and high-performance applications, so developers should follow these C# programming best practices.

5

Advanced Techniques and Patterns

Overview

In Chapter 5: Advanced Techniques and Patterns, a range of advanced concepts and patterns in C# programming are explored, aiming to elevate developers' abilities to create robust and scalable software solutions. As a pivotal strategy for addressing common software design challenges, and maintaining and enhancing scalability, Design Patterns emerge as pivotal strategies in C#. With patterns such as Singleton, Factory, Observer, and Strategy, developers gain reusable solutions that streamline development and improve code organization, ultimately leading to more maintainable and adaptable code. Additionally, Asynchronous Programming Patterns offer strategies for enhancing performance and responsiveness, Dependency Injection and Inversion of Control foster flexibility and maintainability, while Unit Testing and Test-Driven Development ensure that software is of high quality. Developers can deliver high-quality and scalable C# applications efficiently by mastering these advanced techniques and patterns.

Chapter 5: Advanced Techniques and Patterns
Design Patterns in C#

As a powerful tool for solving common software design challenges and promoting maintainability and scalability, Design Patterns in C# take centre stage. As a blueprint for structuring code and achieving flexibility, modularity, and extensibility in applications, design patterns provide developers with reusable solutions to recurring design problems. By leveraging patterns such as Singleton, Factory, Observer, and Strategy, developers can streamline development, improve code organization, and enhance code readability. Through understanding and applying design patterns, developers can create robust, maintainable, and adaptable software solutions for complex systems in C#.

Singleton Pattern

Use the Singleton pattern to ensure that a class has only one instance and can be accessed globally.

```csharp
namespace ZiggyRafiq.CodeExample04;

public class Singleton
{
    private static Singleton _instance;
    private Singleton() { }

    public static Singleton Instance
    {
        get
        {
            if (_instance == null)
            {
                _instance = new Singleton();
            }
```

```
        return _instance;
    }
  }
}
```

Factory Method Pattern

By using the Factory Method pattern, you can create objects without specifying their exact class.

```
namespace ZiggyRafiq.CodeExample04.FactoryMethodPattern;

public interface IProduct
{
    void DisplayInfo();
}

namespace ZiggyRafiq.CodeExample04.FactoryMethodPattern;

public class ConcreteProduct : IProduct
{
    public void DisplayInfo()
    {
        Console.WriteLine("Concrete product info");
    }
}

namespace ZiggyRafiq.CodeExample04.FactoryMethodPattern;

public abstract class Creator
{
    public abstract IProduct FactoryMethod();
}
```

```
namespace ZiggyRafiq.CodeExample04.FactoryMethodPattern;

public class ConcreteCreator : Creator
{
    public override IProduct FactoryMethod()
    {
        return new ConcreteProduct();
    }
}
```

Asynchronous Programming Patterns

In C# applications, Asynchronous Programming Patterns offer strategies for improving performance and responsiveness. Developers can efficiently handle concurrent operations using tools like async/await, Task Parallel Library (TPL), and Reactive Extensions (Rx). By embracing asynchronous programming, application scalability, responsiveness, and resource efficiency are enhanced, resulting in improved user experiences. As a result of proficiency in these patterns, developers can create high-performing, asynchronous C# applications, effectively meeting the challenges of contemporary software development.

Async/Await Pattern

In C#, async/await keywords improve responsiveness and scalability by implementing asynchronous programming patterns.

```
namespace ZiggyRafiq.CodeExample04.AsyncAwaitPattern;

public class Example
{
    public async Task<string> GetDataAsync()
    {
        HttpClient client = new HttpClient();
        return await client.GetStringAsync("https://api.ziggyrafiq.com/data");//please note this is a dead link only used for code example
    }
}
```

Dependency Injection and Inversion of Control

For building flexible and maintainable C# applications, dependency injection and inversion of control are essential concepts. DI promotes loose coupling and facilitates easier testing and swapping implementations by injecting dependencies into a class rather than creating them internally. Rather than managing object creation, IoC containers manage the creation and resolution of dependencies, allowing developers to focus on defining the application's behaviour. As a result of DI and IoC, developers can create modular, extensible, and testable codebases that enhance maintainability and scalability while also encouraging good software design practices in C# applications.

Dependency Injection (DI)
To enable loose coupling and easier testing, inject dependencies from the outside into a class using DI.

```csharp
using Microsoft.Extensions.Logging;

namespace ZiggyRafiq.CodeExample04.DependencyInjection;

public class MyService
{
    private readonly ILogger _logger;

    public MyService(ILogger logger)
    {
        _logger = logger;
    }

    public void DoSomething()
    {
        _logger.LogInformation("Doing something...");
    }
}
```

Inversion of Control (IoC) Container

In large-scale applications, use IoC containers like Autofac or Unity to manage dependencies and facilitate DI.

```csharp
using Autofac;

using Microsoft.Extensions.Logging;

using ZiggyRafiq.CodeExample04.InversionOfControl;


Console.WriteLine("Hello, from Ziggy Rafiq!");


var builder = new ContainerBuilder();


// Register dependencies

builder.RegisterType<ExampleLogger>().As<ILogger>();// Register MyLogger as ILogger

builder.RegisterType<ExampleService>(); // Register MyService


// Build the container

var container = builder.Build();


// Resolve ExampleService from the container

var exampleService = container.Resolve<ExampleService>();


// Use ExampleService

exampleService.DoSomething();
```

The code example above imports Autofac and Microsoft.Extensions.Logging namespaces. Using var builder = new ContainerBuilder();, we create a container builder. We register dependencies using builder.RegisterType<> to associate ExampleLogger with ILogger and ExampleService. We resolve ExampleService from the container after building the container using var container = builder.Build(); By calling exampleService.DoSomething();, we trigger logging of "Doing something..." through the ExampleLogger implementation of ILogger. An IoC container such as Autofac facilitates dependency management and Dependency Injection (DI) in large-scale applications.

Unit Testing and Test-Driven Development

In C# development, unit testing and test-driven development (TDD) are essential practices for ensuring software quality and maintainability. In unit testing, individual units of code are automated tests to verify that they are correct. In TDD, tests are written before the actual code is written, driving the development process. Using these practices, developers can detect bugs early, improve code design, and prevent regressions in the codebase. Unit tests and TDD promote modular, well-structured code, resulting in more robust and maintainable C# applications.

Writing Unit Tests

Create automated tests for individual units of code using unit testing frameworks such as NUnit or MSTest.

```
namespace ZiggyRafiq.CodeExample04.Calculator;

public class CalculatorExample
{
    public int Add(int a, int b)
    {
        return a + b;
    }
}
```

```csharp
using ZiggyRafiq.CodeExample04.Calculator;

namespace ZiggyRafiq.CodeExample04.CalculatorTests;

[TestFixture]
public class CalculatorTests
{
    [Test]
    public void Add_TwoNumbers_ReturnsSum()
    {
        CalculatorExample calculator = new CalculatorExample();
        int result = calculator.Add(3, 5);
        Assert.Equals(8, result);
    }
}
```

Test-Driven Development (TDD)

Writing tests before implementing the corresponding code ensures code correctness and promotes better design.

```csharp
[Test]
public void Add_TwoNumbers_ReturnsSum()
{
    CalculatorExample calculator = new CalculatorExample();
    int result = calculator.Add(3, 5);
    Assert.Equals(8, result);
}
```

As a result of mastering these advanced techniques and patterns in C#, developers can build applications that are more maintainable, scalable, and testable, meeting the demands of modern software development.

6

Integrating with Industry Standards

Overview

In Chapter 6: Integrating with Industry Standards, the focus is on aligning C# applications with prevalent industry norms and regulations. Coding Standards, such as Microsoft Guidelines, ensure consistency, readability, and maintainability, exemplifying best practices. Legal mandates ensure that sensitive data is handled following Industry Regulations, such as GDPR and HIPAA. By implementing interoperability and integration standards, data can be exchanged efficiently with external systems and APIs. Additionally, adhering to accessibility standards and guidelines promotes equal access for individuals with disabilities by ensuring inclusive user experiences. Integrating these standards can ensure regulatory compliance, adhere to coding best practices, and provide accessible and inclusive user experiences, enhancing overall software quality and compliance.

Chapter 6: Integrating with Industry Standards

Compliance with Coding Standards (e.g., Microsoft Guidelines)

Maintain consistency, readability, and maintainability of codebases by following Microsoft's coding guidelines and best practices.

```csharp
// Example of Microsoft coding guideline compliance
namespace ZiggyRafiq.CodeExample05;


public class ExampleClass
{
    public void ExampleMethod()
    {
        Console.WriteLine("Hello from Ziggy Rafiq the author of this book.");
    }
}
```

Conforming to Industry Regulations (e.g., GDPR, HIPAA)

Make sure that sensitive data is handled in accordance with industry regulations such as GDPR (General Data Protection Regulation) and HIPAA (Health Insurance Portability and Accountability Act).

```csharp
// Example of GDPR compliance
using ZiggyRafiq.CodeExample05.Models;

namespace ZiggyRafiq.CodeExample05.Services;

public class UserService
{
    // Delete user data in compliance with GDPR
    public void DeleteUser(User user)
    {
        // Check if user data contains sensitive information
        if (user.ContainsSensitiveInformation)
        {
            // Anonymize or pseudonymize sensitive data
            user.AnonymizeSensitiveInformation();
        }

        // Delete user account
        user.DeleteAccount();
    }
}
```

```csharp
// Example of GDPR compliance
namespace ZiggyRafiq.CodeExample05.Models;

public class User
{
    // Properties
    public Guid Id { get; set; }
    public string Username { get; set; }=string.Empty;
    public string Email { get; set; }= string.Empty;
    public bool ContainsSensitiveInformation { get; set; }

    // Methods
    public void AnonymizeSensitiveInformation()
    {
        // Code to anonymize sensitive information
        if (ContainsSensitiveInformation)
        {
            // Anonymize sensitive data
            Username = "JackUser"; // Example: JackUser
            Email = "jackuser@nodomain.com";
            ContainsSensitiveInformation = false;
        }
    }

    // Delete user data in compliance with GDPR
    public void DeleteAccount()
```

```csharp
{
    // Code to delete user account
    if (Id != Guid.Empty)
    {
        // Perform account deletion process
        Id = Guid.Empty;
        Username = "JackUser";
        Email = "jackuser@nodomain.com";
        ContainsSensitiveInformation = false;
    }
  }
}
```

Interoperability and Integration Standards

Integrate with external systems or APIs in accordance with integration standards to ensure seamless data exchange and communication.

```csharp
// Example of integration with external API
namespace ZiggyRafiq.CodeExample05.Services;


public class ExternalService
{
    public void SendData(string data)
    {
        // Simulate sending data to external API using integration standards
        Console.WriteLine($"Sending data to external API: {data}");
```

```
        // Actual code to send data to external API would go here
    }
}
```

There is a method SendData in this ExternalService class that simulates sending data to an external API. Instead of the Console.WriteLine statement, you would replace it with the actual code to send data to the external API.

Accessibility Standards and Guidelines

Provide equal access to all users, including those with disabilities, by designing and developing applications following accessibility standards and guidelines (e.g., WCAG)

```csharp
// Example of accessibility guideline compliance
namespace ZiggyRafiq.CodeExample05.ViewModels;


public class ImageComponentViewModel
{
    public string ImagePath { get; set; }=string.Empty;
    public string AltText { get; set; } = string.Empty;
}


using Microsoft.AspNetCore.Mvc;
using ZiggyRafiq.CodeExample05.ViewModels;


namespace ZiggyRafiq.CodeExample05.ViewComponents;


public class ImageComponent : ViewComponent
{
```

```csharp
    public IViewComponentResult Invoke(string imagePath, string altText)
    {
        var model = new ImageComponentViewModel
        {
            ImagePath = imagePath,
            AltText = altText
        };

        return View(model);
    }
}

using ZiggyRafiq.CodeExample05.ViewModels;

namespace ZiggyRafiq.CodeExample05.Components;

public class UIComponent
{
    public void Display()
    {
        // Implement UI component with accessibility features
        // For example, ensure proper use of alt text for images is support.

        // Ensure proper alt text for images
        ImageComponentViewModel imageConmpent = new ImageComponentViewModel
```

```
{
    AltText = "Description of the image for screen readers",
    ImagePath = "ImagePath/dummy.jpg"
};

}
}
```

By integrating with industry standards, developers can ensure that their C# applications meet regulatory requirements, adhere to coding best practices, and provide inclusive user experiences, contributing to overall software quality and compliance.

7

Tooling and Automation

Overview

Chapter 7: Tooling and Automation emphasizes optimization of development processes using various tools and automation techniques. A static code analyser, such as ReSharper, SonarQube, or Roslyn Analyzer, identifies issues and vulnerabilities in code. Continuous Integration/Continuous Deployment (CI/CD) Pipelines, such as Jenkins, Azure DevOps, or GitHub Actions, automate build, test, and deployment processes. Code Review Practices, enabled by tools such as GitHub Pull Requests and Azure DevOps Code Review, ensure code quality and compliance with coding standards through collaborative reviews. By automating unit, integration, and end-to-end tests, automated testing frameworks like NUnit and MSTest enhance code reliability. With these tools and automation practices, software developers can streamline workflows, improve code quality, and accelerate software delivery, ultimately increasing productivity and efficiency.

Chapter 7: Tooling and Automation

Code Analysis Tools

Code analysis tools such as ReSharper, SonarQube, and Microsoft Code Analysis Analyzers can be used to perform static code analysis and identify potential issues, code smells, and security vulnerabilities.

```csharp
// Example of using Microsoft.CodeAnalysis.Analyzers
namespace ZiggyRafiq.CodeExample06;
public class ExampleClass
{
    public void ExampleMethod(string input)
    {
        // Potential issue: Unused parameter 'input'
        // Potential issue: Method 'ExampleMethod' is not documented
        // Potential issue: Method 'ExampleMethod' could be made static
        // Potential issue: Variable 'input' is assigned but its value is never used
        Console.WriteLine(input);
    }
}
```

Continuous Integration/Continuous Deployment (CI/CD) Pipelines

Automate build, test, and deployment processes using CI/CD pipelines such as Jenkins, Azure DevOps, or GitHub Actions to ensure rapid, reliable delivery of software updates.

```
# Example of CI/CD pipeline configuration using GitHub Actions
```

```yaml
name: CI/CD

on:
  push:
    branches:
      - main

jobs:
  build:
    runs-on: ubuntu-latest

    steps:
    - name: Checkout repository
      uses: actions/checkout@v2


    - name: Build and test
      run: |
        dotnet build
        dotnet test
```

Code Review Practices and Tools

Establish code review practices within the development team to ensure code quality, knowledge sharing, and coding standards compliance.

```csharp
namespace ZiggyRafiq.CodeExample06;

// Example of code review comments

public class CodeReviewExample
{
    public void CodeReviewMethod()
    {
        // Code with review comments

        // Comment: Consider using descriptive method and variable names for better readability.
        int x = 10;
        int y = 20;

        // Comment: This loop can be optimized for better performance.
        for (int i = 0; i < 100; i++)
        {
            // Code here...
        }

        // Comment: Ensure proper exception handling is implemented to handle potential errors.
        try
        {
            // Code here...
        }
```

```
        catch (Exception ex)
        {
            // Code here...
        }
    }
}
```

The code in this example above contains comments highlighting areas that need to be improved during code review. As a result of these comments, the developer is provided with actionable feedback, which improves code quality and adherence to coding standards. As a result of incorporating code review practices and tools like these into your development workflow, your software will be more robust and maintainable.

Code review tools such as GitHub Pull Requests, GitLab Merge Requests, and Azure DevOps Code Review can facilitate collaborative code reviews and provide developers with feedback.

Automated Testing Frameworks

Use automated testing frameworks such as NUnit, MSTest, or xUnit.net to automate unit, integration, and end-to-end tests.

```
namespace ZiggyRafiq.CodeExample06;

public class Calculator

{

    public int Add(int a, int b)

    {

        return a + b;

    }


    public int Subtract(int a, int b)

    {

        return a - b;

    }


    public int Multiply(int a, int b)

    {

        return a * b;

    }


    public int Divide(int a, int b)

    {

        if (b == 0)

        {

            throw new ArgumentException("Divisor cannot be zero.", nameof(b));
```

```csharp
        }

        return a / b;
    }
}

// Example of xUnit.net test fixture
namespace ZiggyRafiq.CodeExample06.CalculatorTests
{
    public class CalculatorTests
    {
        [Fact]
        public void Add_TwoNumbers_ReturnsSum()
        {
            // Arrange
            Calculator calculator = new Calculator();

            // Act
            int result = calculator.Add(3, 5);

            // Assert
            Assert.Equal(8, result);
        }
    }
}
```

The test fixture "CalculatorTests" contains the unit test method "Add_TwoNumbers_ReturnsSum". The [Fact] attribute is used by the xUnit.net test runner to execute the method as a test case. In an Arrange-Act-Assert (AAA) test method, preconditions and inputs are defined (Arrange), the method under test is invoked (Act), and the outcome is verified (Assert). Automated testing frameworks such as xUnit.net help developers streamline test writing and execution, facilitating early bug detection and boosting code reliability.

Software developers can streamline development workflows, improve code quality, and accelerate delivery of software products by leveraging tooling and automation practices.

8

Collaborative Development Practices

Overview

Collaboration and teamwork within development teams are the focus of Chapter 8: Collaborative Development Practices. To ensure traceability and collaboration, Version Control Best Practices recommend meaningful commit messages, branching strategies, and frequent commits. In code review processes, quality, correctness, and conformance to standards are stressed. The Pair Programming and Mob Programming techniques facilitate collaborative coding sessions where developers exchange knowledge and ensure code quality. Software development practices such as Scrum and Kanban foster collaboration, transparency, and iterative development. Teams can improve communication, and teamwork, and ultimately deliver more effective software products by implementing these collaborative development practices.

Chapter 8: Collaborative Development Practices

Version Control Best Practices

To ensure traceability and collaboration within the development team, follow version control best practices such as meaningful commit messages, branching strategies, and frequent commits.

```
# Example of meaningful commit message

git commit -m "Add feature to handle user authentication"
```

Code Review Processes

Create code review processes where developers submit their code changes for peer review, focusing on code quality, correctness, and adherence to standards.

```csharp
// Example of code review comment

namespace ZiggyRafiq.CodeExamples07;


public class CodeReviewCommentExampleClass
{
    public void ExampleMethod()
    {
        // Code with review comment

        // Comment: Consider refactoring this method into smaller, more focused functions for better readability and maintainability.

        // Example: private int CalculateTotal(int[] values) { ... }

        // Example: private void DisplayResult(int result) { ... }
    }
}
```

```
}
```

A code review comment is provided within the ExampleMethod of the CodeReviewCommentExampleClass class in this code example above. As a result of the comment, the developer is advised to consider refactoring the method into smaller, more focused functions in order to improve readability and maintainability of the code. Development teams can collaborate effectively to produce high-quality code by implementing code review processes and incorporating constructive feedback like this.

Pair Programming and Mob Programming

By using pair programming and mob programming techniques, developers collaborate in pairs or groups to write code together, share knowledge, and ensure better code quality.

```
// Example of pair programming session
namespace ZiggyRafiq.CodeExamples07
{
    public class PairProgrammingExampleClass
    {
        public void ExampleMethod()
        {
            // Code written collaboratively by two developers

            // Developer 1
            // Code here...

            // Developer 2
            // Code here...
```

```
        // Discussion and collaboration between developers to write and review code
    }
  }
}
```

In this code example above, developers collaborate in pairs to write code within the ExampleMethod of the PairProgrammingExampleClass class. Each developer contributes to the code, discussing and reviewing each other's work in real-time. As a result of pair programming and mob programming, teamwork, knowledge sharing, and collective ownership of code are enhanced, leading to improved solutions and quality code.

Agile Development Practices

To foster collaboration, transparency, and iterative software delivery, embrace Agile development practices like Scrum and Kanban.

Using Agile development practices, teams prioritize collaboration, transparency, and iterative software development. Teams can respond quickly to change, deliver value incrementally, and ensure continuous improvement by adopting Agile principles. Using this documentation, you can learn how to implement Agile practices such as Scrum and Kanban.

Scrum

Several key components make up Scrum, an Agile framework that emphasizes iterative development, regular feedback, and continuous improvement.

Roles
- **Product Owner**: Defining the product backlog and representing stakeholders.
- **Scrum Master**: Ensures adherence to Scrum principles and facilitates the Scrum process.
- **Development Team**: A self-organizing cross-functional team responsible for delivering working software in increments.

Artifacts
- **Product Backlog**: List of user stories, features, and enhancements prioritized.

- **Sprint Backlog**: Items selected for implementation during a sprint from the product backlog.
- **Increment**: Software functionality completed during a sprint.

Events
- **Sprint Planning:** A collaborative session to plan the upcoming sprint.
- **Daily Standup:** A daily meeting where team members discuss progress and synchronize their activities.
- **Sprint Review:** Presenting the completed work to stakeholders and gathering feedback.
- **Sprint Retrospective:** Analyzing the sprint process to identify improvements.

Kanban

Kanban is a visual management method that emphasizes flow, limiting work in progress, and continuous delivery.
- **Visualization**: Kanban boards are used to visualize work items and represent workflows.
- **Work in Progress (WIP) Limits**: Limiting the number of work items allowed at each stage of the workflow to optimize flow.
- **Pull System**: Work is pulled into the next stage of the workflow only when capacity permits.

Software development efforts can be enhanced by embracing Agile practices like Scrum and Kanban, which promote collaboration, transparency, and adaptability. Through iterative delivery, frequent feedback, and continuous improvement, teams can deliver value more effectively and efficiently to customers.

The implementation of collaborative development practices can lead to improved communication, teamwork, and ultimately more effective software products that meet the needs of stakeholders.

9

Collaborative Development Practices

Overview

During Chapter 9, methods and strategies are presented to enhance teamwork, communication, and productivity within software development teams. For efficient collaboration, traceability, and code management, Version Control Best Practices emphasize using systems such as Git, with key practices such as regular commits, descriptive messages, and following branching strategies. By conducting systematic reviews, providing feedback, and detecting errors, Code Review Processes promote knowledge sharing and consistency and ensure code quality and standards compliance. By fostering real-time collaboration and knowledge exchange among developers, Pair Programming and Mob Programming improve code quality and team cohesion. Agile Development Practices, such as Scrum and Kanban, emphasize iterative delivery, transparency, and adaptive planning, enabling teams to respond effectively to changing requirements and deliver value incrementally. Team members can create high-quality software products that meet customer expectations and deliver value efficiently by embracing these collaborative practices.

Chapter 9: Collaborative Development Practices

Version Control Best Practices
Within development teams, Version Control Best Practices ensure efficient collaboration, traceability, and code management. In addition to facilitating collaboration among multiple developers on the same project, version control systems (VCS) like Git help teams track changes to their codebase over time. The following benefits can be achieved by following version control best practices:

Traceability
A version control system keeps track of all changes to the codebase, including who made them and when they were made. This traceability is crucial for understanding the evolution of the codebase, identifying problems, and ensuring accountability.

Collaboration
Multiple developers can work on the same codebase concurrently with version control systems without interfering with each other's work. Developers can collaborate effectively on various features or bug fixes while keeping the main codebase stable with features such as branching and merging.

Code Quality
Version control systems help maintain code quality and consistency by enforcing best practices, such as meaningful commit messages and code review processes. As a result of code reviews, developers can provide feedback, catch errors early, and adhere to coding standards.

Commit Regularly
Encourage team members to commit changes regularly to the version control system to facilitate collaboration and minimise conflict.

Use Descriptive Commit Messages
Write clear and descriptive commit messages that summarize the changes made in each commit, so team members can understand what each commit is about.

Follow Branching Strategies
Develop a branching strategy, such as GitFlow, to manage releases, hotfixes, and feature development effectively, ensuring a structured and organized process.

Following these guidelines can help developers use version control systems effectively and adhere to best practices.

Meaningful Commit Messages
Describe the changes in a meaningful manner in each commit message. Meaningful commit messages facilitate code review and troubleshooting by making it easier to understand the purpose of each change.

Branching Strategies
Implement a branching strategy that suits the team's workflow, such as GitFlow or trunk-based development. Branching strategies define how code changes are managed, merged, and deployed.

Frequent Commits
Make small, incremental commits instead of large, monolithic ones. This enables changes to be tracked consistently and reduces the possibility of conflicts when merging branches.

Code Review Processes
Implement code review processes to ensure coding standards are adhered to and knowledge is shared within the team. Code reviews help catch errors, ensure coding standards are adhered to, and promote knowledge sharing among team members.

Using these version control best practices, development teams can streamline collaboration, maintain code quality, and deliver high-quality software products quickly.

Code Review Processes
Within development teams, code review processes ensure code quality, correctness, and compliance with standards. As part of a code review, members of the team systematically examine changes to the codebase, provide feedback, identify potential issues, and verify compliance with coding guidelines. These processes offer several benefits, as listed below.

Quality Assurance
Code reviews serve as an additional layer of quality assurance, allowing developers to identify errors, bugs, and potential security vulnerabilities before they are merged into the main codebase. Team members contribute to code quality and reliability by reviewing each other's code.

Knowledge Sharing
During code reviews, junior developers can learn from more experienced colleagues by receiving feedback and insights into best practices, coding techniques, and design patterns.

Consistency
By enforcing coding standards and best practices during code reviews, teams ensure that the codebase remains cohesive and comprehensible to all members.

Following these best practices will help teams conduct effective code reviews.

Define Review Criteria
Defining Review Criteria: Establish clear criteria for determining whether a code review has been successful, such as functionality, performance, security, and compliance with coding standards. It is easier to streamline the review process and ensure consistent feedback if you have predefined review criteria.

Assign Reviewers
Assign reviewers to each code change based on their expertise and familiarity with the relevant codebase. Reviewers should have a good understanding of the project requirements and coding standards.

Use Review Tools
Facilitate collaborative reviews by using code review tools such as GitHub Pull Requests, GitLab Merge Requests, and Azure DevOps Code Review. Using these tools, you can comment, discuss, and approve code changes, improving the efficiency and transparency of the review process.

Establish Guidelines
To ensure consistency and effectiveness in the review process, establish guidelines outlining the expectations, criteria, and responsibilities of both reviewers and authors.

Provide Constructive Feedback
Promote a culture of continuous improvement by encouraging reviewers to offer constructive feedback that focuses on code quality, readability and maintainability, as well as adherence to coding standards.

Utilize Code Review Tools
To facilitate asynchronous code reviews, streamline the code review process, and keep track of feedback, utilize code review tools such as GitHub Pull Requests or Bitbucket Code Insights.

Provide Constructive Feedback
You should provide constructive feedback that is specific, actionable, and respectful. Your feedback should focus on improving the code's clarity, functionality, and maintainability rather than criticizing the developer personally.

As a result of incorporating code review processes into their development workflow, teams can foster a culture of continuous improvement, collaboration, and excellence that results in higher-quality software products.

Pair Programming and Mob Programming
There are several advantages to pair and mob programming, which are collaborative development practices in which developers write code together in pairs or in groups.

Knowledge Sharing
Using pair programming and mob programming, team members can exchange ideas, share expertise, and learn from each other's experiences. By working together closely, developers can exchange ideas, share expertise, and learn from each other. As junior developers work with more experienced colleagues, senior developers gain new perspectives.

Enhanced Code Quality
By identifying errors, bugs, and potential improvements with multiple eyes, pair programming and mob programming enhance code quality more effectively than individual coding. Before integrating code into the main codebase, developers can identify issues early, discuss alternative approaches, and ensure it meets quality standards.

Improved Collaboration
In the development team, pair programming and mob programming improve collaboration and teamwork. In real-time, developers can brainstorm solutions, resolve challenges, and make collective decisions, resulting in more successful outcomes and stronger team cohesion.

The following best practices should be considered by teams when leveraging pair programming and mob programming:

Rotate Roles
To ensure balanced participation and to prevent fatigue, rotate roles between the driver (the one writing code) and the navigator (the one reviewing and providing feedback). Rotating roles allows all team members to contribute ideas and insights effectively.

Establish Clear Goals
To maximize productivity, define clear goals for each pairing or mob session. Clearly communicate the tasks to be accomplished, the expected results, and any constraints or deadlines.

Encourage Communication
Facilitate open communication and active participation between team members during pairing and mobbing sessions. Encourage developers to ask questions, share ideas, and express concerns freely.

Use Collaboration Tools
To facilitate communication and collaboration with distributed teams or remote work environments, use collaboration tools such as screen sharing, code sharing, and virtual whiteboards. You can collaborate and share code in real time with tools like VS Code Live Share or Zoom.

Pair Programming
In pair programming, two developers take turns writing code and reviewing each other's work in real time, promoting collaboration, knowledge sharing, and code quality.

Mob Programming
Take part in mob programming, where the entire team works together on the same task at the same time, rotating roles frequently, encouraging collective ownership, creativity, and problem-solving.

With pair programming and mob programming as part of their development practices, teams can harness the collective intelligence and creativity of their members, resulting in higher-quality code, faster problem resolution, and a more cohesive team.

Agile Development Practices
Software development teams use agile development practices, such as Scrum and Kanban, to foster collaboration, transparency, and iterative software delivery. As explained below, these practices offer several benefits.

Flexibility
The agile methodology emphasizes adaptability and responsiveness to change. Teams can adjust priorities, requirements, and project plans based on feedback and evolving business needs, allowing for more flexible and dynamic development.

Transparency
Providing stakeholders with visibility into the development process and progress is one of the ways Agile practices promote transparency. In addition to sharing updates, discussing challenges, and aligning on goals, team members also hold regular meetings, such as sprint reviews and daily stand-ups, fostering trust and accountability.

Iterative Delivery
The agile development process is iterative, meaning work is divided into manageable increments known as iterations or sprints, which allow teams to deliver working software incrementally, allowing stakeholders to provide feedback early and often, improving requirements validation and reducing project failure risk.

Teams should consider the following best practices when implementing Agile development practices:

Define Clear Objectives
Set Clear Objectives: To ensure that the team understands the desired outcomes and success criteria, make sure that project goals, objectives, and priorities are clearly defined at the beginning. To capture requirements and define scope, use techniques such as user stories and acceptance criteria.

Embrace Empirical Process Control
To optimize delivery, Agile methodologies are based on empirical process control, which emphasizes transparency, inspection, and adaptation. Regularly inspect the progress of the work and adapt plans and processes based on feedback and lessons learned.

Foster Cross-Functional Teams
Build cross-functional teams consisting of developers, testers, designers, and product owners with a variety of skills and expertise. By collaborating cross-functionally, sharing knowledge, and taking collective ownership of project outcomes, cross-functional teams can work more effectively.

Iterate and Improve
The team should continuously reflect on their performance and identify areas for improvement. Conduct retrospective meetings at the end of each sprint to discuss what went well, what could be improved, and actionable steps for enhancing team effectiveness and efficiency.

Embrace Agile Principles
Use Agile principles such as iterative development, customer collaboration, and responding to change to deliver value incrementally and adapt to changing requirements.

Scrum Framework
Using the Scrum framework, conduct regular sprint cycles, sprint planning, daily stand-up meetings, sprint reviews, and retrospectives to foster teamwork, transparency, and continuous improvement.

Kanban Method
Apply the Kanban method to visualize workflow, limit work in progress (WIP), and optimize the flow of work, allowing teams to prioritize tasks, identify bottlenecks, and deliver value more efficiently.

Through these collaborative development practices, teams can create top-notch software products that align with customer expectations and business goals, while also improving teamwork and communication. By embracing Agile development methodologies, teams can deliver high-quality software products quickly, adapt quickly to market changes, and ultimately deliver greater value to stakeholders.

10
Case Studies and Examples

Overview

To provide valuable insights for developers, Chapter 10: Case Studies and Examples examines real-world scenarios in C# development, analysing both good and bad practices. Developers can gain a deeper understanding of coding techniques, methodologies, and industry standards by utilizing real-world examples. As part of refactoring exercises, developers can improve code quality and foster a culture of continuous improvement within their teams. In addition, performance optimization case studies provide developers with the knowledge and tools they need to enhance application performance effectively by identifying bottlenecks, implementing optimization techniques, and promoting scalability planning. Providing practical guidance and fostering critical thinking, this chapter empowers developers to deliver better software solutions and maximize their impact.

Chapter 10: Case Studies and Examples

Real-world Examples of Good and Bad Practices
C# development examples of good and bad practices serve as practical examples of coding techniques, methodologies, and approaches that are effective and ineffective. These examples offer valuable insights into industry standards, best practices, and common pitfalls encountered during software development. Developers gain a deeper understanding of how to write robust, maintainable code by examining both good and bad practices.

Why Use Real-world Examples
Learning Opportunities
Developers can learn from real-world examples by analysing, dissecting, and analysing real-world scenarios, providing tangible lessons that go beyond theoretical knowledge.

Illustration of Concepts
Using examples to illustrate abstract concepts makes them more accessible and relatable by showing how to apply them in real-world scenarios.

Identifying Patterns
Identifying patterns helps developers replicate successful approaches and avoid repeating mistakes by analysing good and bad practices.

Encouraging Critical Thinking
Providing contrasting examples helps developers foster a mindset of continuous improvement and refinement by thinking critically about their code.

How to Use the Real-world Examples
How to Use Real-world Examples of Good and Bad Practices:

Case Studies
Demonstrate how good and bad practices are applied in different scenarios, highlighting their outcomes and lessons learned.

Code Samples
Provide snippets of code representing both good and bad practices, along with reasons for their effectiveness or ineffectiveness.

Discussion Forums
Encourage developers to share their own experiences and insights regarding good and bad practices in discussions within development teams or online forums.

Training Workshops
Develop training workshops where developers analyse real-world examples collaboratively, discussing their implications, and brainstorming alternative solutions.

Continuous Integration
Use automated tools to detect and flag instances of bad practices in continuous integration using real-world examples.

Good Practice
Display real-world examples of well-designed, maintainable, and scalable software systems that conform to coding standards, design patterns, and architecture best practices.

Projects that demonstrate collaboration, Agile methodologies, and compliance with industry standards and regulations should be highlighted.

Bad Practices
Learn how to detect and avoid pitfalls such as tight coupling, spaghetti code, and lack of documentation in poorly designed, unmaintainable, and insecure software systems.

Provide examples of the consequences of poor practices, such as technical debt, maintenance costs, and security vulnerabilities, emphasizing the need to adhere to best practices.

By providing practical guidance, fostering critical thinking, and promoting continuous improvement in C# development, real-world examples of good and bad practices serve as valuable educational resources. Developers can enhance their coding skills, enhance code quality, and deliver better software solutions by effectively leveraging these examples.

Refactoring Exercises

Through refactoring exercises, developers are able to improve existing code while preserving its functionality while improving its design, structure, and readability. To improve maintainability, performance, and scalability, these exercises involve identifying areas of code that could be enhanced, refactored, or optimized. Developers gain practical experience in applying refactoring techniques and principles to real-world codebases through refactoring exercises, enhancing their skills and deepening their understanding of software design.

Why Use Refactoring Exercises
Skill Development
Developing refactoring skills helps developers become more proficient at restructuring and improving code by performing refactoring exercises.

Code Quality Improvement
By systematically refactoring code, developers can improve its quality, making it easier to understand, maintain, and extend.

Performance Optimization
By eliminating inefficiencies, reducing code duplication, and optimizing algorithms, refactoring can lead to performance improvements.

Risk Mitigation
Refactoring exercises provide a controlled environment for experimenting with code changes, reducing the risk of introducing bugs or regressions into production.

Continuous Learning
Refactoring exercises foster collaboration and knowledge sharing within development teams by encouraging continuous learning and improvement.

How to Use Refactoring Exercises
Identify Target Code
Choose code sections in existing projects or code bases that can be refactored. These sections may have poor design, excessive complexity, or duplication.

Analyse Code Smells
Use code smells to detect refactoring needs. Code smells include duplicated code, long methods, large classes, and excessive nesting.

Apply Refactoring Techniques
Use refactoring techniques to solve identified code smells, such as extracting methods, consolidating conditional expressions, and introducing polymorphism.

Document Changes
Ensure clarity and transparency for other team members and future reference by documenting the rationale behind each refactoring decision.

Test Changes
After applying refactoring changes, thoroughly test the modified code to ensure that its behaviour remains consistent with the original. Automated tests can help detect regressions.

Review and Reflect
To share insights, review and reflect on the results of the refactoring exercises, and identify opportunities for further improvement, conduct code reviews and retrospectives.

Finally, refactoring exercises are a practical and effective way to improve code quality, enhance developer skills, and create a culture of continuous improvement in development teams. Developers can make meaningful improvements to software projects by incorporating refactoring exercises into their workflows, resulting in more robust, maintainable solutions in the end.

Identify Code Smells
Display code snippets that contain common code smells, such as duplicated code, long methods, and inappropriate naming conventions.

Refactoring Techniques
Demonstrate refactoring techniques including extracting methods, renaming variables, and introducing design patterns to improve code readability, maintainability, and performance.

Before-and-After Examples
Examples of Before-and-After Refactoring: Show how poorly structured code can be transformed into cleaner, more maintainable code using before-and-after examples.

Performance Optimization Case Studies
In Performance Optimization Case Studies, software applications are analysed and optimized for speed, efficiency, and resource utilization. In these case studies, performance bottlenecks are identified, optimizations are implemented, and performance impacts are measured. Developers gain insight into common performance issues and learn effective strategies for improving application responsiveness and scalability by examining real-world scenarios.

Why Use Performance Optimization Case Studies
Identifying performance bottlenecks such as slow database queries, inefficient algorithms, and resource-intensive operations is one of the many benefits of performance optimization case studies. Additionally, they provide hands-on experience in diagnosing and resolving performance problems, optimizing techniques, and measuring performance improvements. Thirdly, developers gain practical insights into application performance by analysing real-world examples, such as database access patterns, network latency, and resource contention, among others. Moreover, these case studies encourage a culture of continuous improvement within development teams, encouraging proactive identification and resolution of performance bottlenecks. Finally, they facilitate scalability planning, providing developers with the tools they need to develop scalable solutions capable of handling increasing workloads and user demands. In general, performance optimization case studies contribute to improving application performance and fostering a culture of improvement within development teams.

Identifying Bottlenecks
Case studies provide opportunities for identifying common performance bottlenecks, such as slow database queries, inefficient algorithms, and resource-intensive operations.

Hands-on Experience
The developer gains hands-on experience diagnosing and resolving performance issues, optimizing techniques, and measuring performance improvements.

Practical Insights
Developers gain practical insights into application performance by examining real-world examples, such as database access patterns, network latency, and resource contention.

Continuous Improvement
Performance optimization case studies promote a culture of continuous improvement within development teams, encouraging developers to identify and address performance bottlenecks proactively.

Scalability Planning
Through case studies, developers learn how to design and implement scalable solutions that can handle increasing workloads and user demands.

How to Use Performance Optimization Case Studies
The first step in using performance optimization case studies effectively is identifying performance metrics such as response time, throughput, and resource utilization to evaluate the impact of optimizations. They need specialized tools to analyse application performance to identify bottlenecks, such as CPU-intensive methods, memory leaks, or slow database queries. Analysing performance data is used to identify root causes of issues and prioritize optimizations. To measure performance improvements after implementation using optimization techniques such as algorithmic improvements and caching, benchmarks and load tests are essential. Documenting findings and sharing insights with team members ensures collective understanding and learning. To achieve sustained improvements over time, developers should continuously iterate and refine their optimizations. Enhancing the performance of software applications involves identifying bottlenecks, implementing optimization strategies, and benchmarking the results.

Identify Performance Metrics
Measure performance before and after optimization by identifying key performance metrics, such as response time, throughput, and resource utilization.

Profile Application Performance
Utilize profiling tools to find performance bottlenecks and hotspots within the application, such as CPU-intensive methods, memory leaks, and slow database queries.

Analyse Performance Data
Analyse performance data to identify root causes of performance issues and prioritize optimizations based on their impact.

Implement Optimizations
To address identified performance bottlenecks, implement optimization techniques such as algorithmic improvements, caching, asynchronous processing, and database query optimization.

Measure Performance Improvements
Measure the impact of optimizations on application performance by comparing performance metrics before and after optimizations. Simulate real-world scenarios with benchmarks and load tests.

Document Findings
Share knowledge and insights with other team members and stakeholders by documenting the case study findings, optimizations applied, and performance improvements achieved.

Iterate and Refine
Continually monitor application performance and iterate on optimizations to further improve performance over time. Performance optimization is a continuous process that requires regular monitoring and refinement.

Identify Bottlenecks
Assess the impact of performance bottlenecks in software applications on user experience or system efficiency based on real-world scenarios.

Optimization Strategies
Identify strategies for optimizing performance, including algorithmic improvements, caching mechanisms, and database indexing.

Benchmarking Results
Present benchmark results before and after performance optimization efforts to demonstrate the improvements made in response time, throughput, or resource utilization.

By studying performance optimization case studies, developers gain valuable insight into real-world challenges and solutions, enabling them to adopt best practices, refactor legacy codebases, and improve performance. By participating in these studies, developers will be able to gain practical experience in diagnosing, addressing, and preventing software performance problems. By implementing optimization techniques and measuring performance improvements in real-world scenarios, developers can increase the speed, efficiency, and scalability of their applications, resulting in a better user experience and maximizing the value of their software solutions.

11

Future Trends and Evolving Standard

Overview

A comprehensive look at future trends and evolving standards within the C# ecosystem is provided in Chapter 11: Future Trends and Evolving Standards. Developers can anticipate enhanced performance, cross-platform capabilities, and enhanced development experiences based on the advancements in .NET 6, Blazor, and WebAssembly for web applications, and cloud-native development trends. Additionally, the need for adaptability and continuous learning is underscored by the potential changes in coding standards and practices, including the shift towards functional programming, emphasis on clean code principles, and the adoption of AI and machine learning technologies. In a rapidly changing digital landscape, C# developers can drive innovation and success by embracing Agile and DevOps practices and integrating ethical and responsible AI.

Chapter 11: Future Trends and Evolving Standard

Emerging Technologies in C# Ecosystem
As developers explore emerging technologies within the C# ecosystem, they can expect exciting prospects. Developers can look forward to improved performance, cross-platform capabilities, and innovative language features with .NET 6 and beyond. In addition to streamlining development processes and offering rich user experiences, developers can craft interactive client-side web applications with Blazor and WebAssembly using C# and . NET. A developer can also build scalable and resilient cloud applications easily by embracing cloud-native development trends like serverless computing, containerization, and microservice architecture. By embracing these emerging technologies, C# developers can stay at the forefront of innovation and deliver cutting-edge solutions to meet changing industry demands.

NET 6 and Beyond
.Net 6 and Beyond: Discover the latest advancements in the .NET ecosystem, including enhanced performance, cross-platform capabilities, and new language capabilities in the future versions of .NET 6.

Blazor and WebAssembly
Develop interactive client-side web applications using C# and .NET with Blazor and WebAssembly.

Cloud-Native Development
Using C#, learn about new trends in cloud-native development, such as serverless computing, containerization, and microservice architecture that enable scalable and resilient cloud applications.

Potential Changes in Coding Standards and Practices
C# developers face a dynamic landscape when they anticipate potential changes in coding standards and practices. As a result of the increased interest in paradigms influenced by languages such as F# and the inclusion of functional features in C#, functional programming has become increasingly popular. To ensure simplicity, readability, and maintainability in evolving software complexity, clean code principles, such as SOLID, DRY, and YAGNI, become paramount. Furthermore, the adoption of AI and machine learning technologies, facilitated by frameworks like ML.NET,

opens the door for developers to build intelligent applications and automate tasks, paving the way for a new era of innovation and efficiency. With these changes in mind, C# developers can remain agile, responsive, and adept at leveraging emerging technologies to deliver impactful solutions in a rapidly changing digital environment.

Shift towards Functional Programming
Focus on Functional Programming: Discuss the growing interest in functional programming paradigms in the C# community, influenced by languages like F# and the adoption of functional features in C#.

Emphasis on Clean Code Principles
Emphasize the importance of clean code principles such as **SOLID**, **DRY**, and **YAGNI**, advocating for simpler, more readable, and maintainable codebases as software complexity evolves.

Adoption of AI and Machine Learning
Through frameworks like ML.NET, developers can build intelligent applications and automate tasks using AI and machine learning technologies.

Adapting to Future Industry Trends
For C# developers to effectively navigate evolving technologies and market demands, they must take a proactive approach, emphasizing continuous learning and upskilling. In an ever-changing environment, developers can remain agile and responsive by staying abreast of new tools, frameworks, and methodologies. Investing in Agile and DevOps practices fosters collaboration, automation, and rapid delivery cycles, allowing organizations to meet customer demands quickly. In addition, embracing ethical and responsible AI practices is essential, ensuring ethical decision-making frameworks and responsible development practices are integrated into AI and machine learning technologies. Developers in C# can position themselves at the forefront of industry trends and standards if they embrace these principles and drive innovation and success.

Continuous Learning and Upskilling
Emphasize the importance of continuous learning and upskilling to stay on top of evolving technologies and industry trends, encouraging developers to explore new tools, frameworks, and methodologies.

Agile and DevOps Practices
Invest in Agile and DevOps practices to enable organizations to respond quickly to changing market demands and deliver value to customers by promoting collaboration, automation, and rapid delivery cycles.

Ethical and Responsible AI
Embrace ethical and responsible AI practices, emphasizing the importance of ethical decision-making frameworks and responsible AI development practices when integrating AI and machine learning technologies.

C# developers can adapt coding practices, embrace new technologies, and align with industry trends to drive innovation and success by anticipating future trends and evolving standards.

12
Wrapping Up

Overview

As a comprehensive conclusion to the journey through C# development, Chapter 12: Wrapping Up provides developers with critical insights and essential practices. To ensure a clean, maintainable, and efficient code base, it is important to follow coding standards and best practices. Additionally, adopting collaborative development practices such as code reviews, pair programming, and Agile methodologies enhances teamwork and improves code quality. To remain competitive and future-proof their skills in the ever-evolving technology landscape, developers need to remain informed and adaptable to emerging trends and industry advancements. Finally, continuous improvement and learning are emphasized throughout the software development lifecycle as a means of prioritizing code quality. Moreover, developers are encouraged to explore further resources to enhance their knowledge and skills in C# development, collaborative practices, and emerging technologies. To conclude, the chapter emphasizes the importance of technical proficiency, collaboration, and continuous learning in mastering C# development, to contribute to building robust and future-proof software.

Chapter 12: Wrapping Up

Recap of Key Takeaways
Recapitulating the key takeaways from this chapter emphasizes the essential aspects critical to successful C# development. For clean, maintainable, and efficient code, it's imperative to follow coding standards and adhere to best practices. In addition, embracing collaborative development practices such as code reviews, pair programming, and Agile methodologies improves teamwork and results in better quality code. Finally, developers must remain adaptable and informed about emerging trends, evolving standards, and industry advancements to stay competitive and future-proof their skills in the ever-evolving technology landscape. Developers can navigate C# development effectively and confidently by internalizing these key insights.

Coding Standards and Best Practices
Writing clean, maintainable, and efficient code in C# requires adhering to coding standards and best practices.

Collaborative Development
Discuss the benefits of collaborative development practices such as code reviews, pair programming, and Agile methodologies for improving teamwork and code quality.

Adaptation to Future Trends
To remain competitive and future-proof their skills, developers should keep abreast of emerging technologies, evolving standards, and industry trends.

Final Thoughts on Achieving Code Quality
To ensure code quality is prioritized throughout the entire software development lifecycle, from initial design to deployment and maintenance, emphasize this importance. To deliver high-quality software solutions that meet the needs of users and stakeholders effectively, encourage developers to constantly strive for improvement, embrace feedback, and seek opportunities for learning and growth.

Resources for Further Learning

Support developers in advancing their knowledge and skills in C# development, coding standards, collaborative practices, and emerging technologies by providing a curated list of resources, including books, online courses, documentation, and community forums. To stay up to date with industry trends and best practices, developers should explore these resources to gain practical insights, expand their understanding, and gain practical insights.

This book concludes by emphasizing the importance of technical proficiency, collaboration, and continual learning in mastering C# development. As technology continues to evolve, developers can contribute to building robust, maintainable, future-proof software solutions by following coding standards, embracing collaborative practices, and staying up to date on emerging trends.

www.ingramcontent.com/pod-product-compliance
Lightning Source LLC
Chambersburg PA
CBHW070155230526
45471CB00002B/676